D1394783

THE STORY OF

TOMÁS
Mac CURTÁIN

Irish Heroes for Children

THE STORY OF

TOMÁS Mac CURTÁIN

FIONNUALA Mac CURTAIN

MERCIER PRESS

IRISH PUBLISHER – IRISH STORY

MERCIER PRESS

Cork

www.mercierpress.ie

© Fionnuala Mac Curtain, 2011

ISBN: 978 1 85635 716 6

10 9 8 7 6 5 4 3 2 1

A CIP record for this title is available from the British Library

Printed and bound in the EU.

CONTENTS

Introduction

Whispers of 'the Lord Mayor is dead' spread over the city of Cork.

What began as a rumour at about 2 a.m. became a confirmed fact as the morning came. There was very little information available – masked, armed men had broken into the Lord Mayor's home at approximately 1.15 a.m., pushed his pregnant wife out of the way and shot him through the heart at his bedroom door. The gun was fired at point blank range. His wife and young children witnessed the scene.

All the people of Cork city were overcome with grief and disbelief. Tomás Mac Curtáin had only held the office of Lord Mayor for fifty days, and now he was dead. An outrageous act of murder had taken place in their city.

Tomás's last words were, 'Into thy hands O Lord I commend my spirit.' His wife Elizabeth watched as her husband took his last breath and she whispered to him, 'Remember darling, it's all for Ireland.'

It was the morning of his thirty-sixth birthday.

Tomás's story begins many years earlier, near Mallow, when Patrick Curtin married Julia Sheehan. They had a large family and it was a very happy and busy household. On 20 March 1884, Tom Curtin was born at Ballyknockane. Tommy, as he was affectionately called as a baby, was the youngest of twelve children and was spoiled by everyone from birth. He inherited his parent's passion for learning and their deep love of the Irish language, music and

He inherited his parent's passion for learning and their deep love of the Irish language, music and history.

history. At the age of thirteen, when Tom finished at Burnfort School and many of his classmates were going out to work, he took the opportunity to keep up his studies by moving into the city of Cork. He went to live with his sister Mary, known as Minnie, who was married to Bill Twomey. The couple had no children and welcomed Tom warmly.

The Twomey's house at 68 Great Britain Street became Tom's new home and he went to the North Monastery secondary school. There he became close friends with an older student, Terence MacSwiney, who was usually called Terry Mac. The two boys were very different, but they became best friends and were always talking and playing together. Tom studied very hard at the North Monastery. He got excellent marks in many subjects and when it came to Irish and history he read so much he knew almost as much as many of his teachers.

Another of Tom's friends, Con Collins, took him to a Gaelic League meeting in Blackpool in 1901. The Gaelic League had been founded in 1893 to try and make sure that the Irish language would

The Gaelic League had been founded in 1893 to try and make sure that the Irish language would continue to be spoken in Ireland.

continue to be spoken in Ireland. At the time, English was the language used in schools and was becoming more and more common as the language spoken in Ireland generally. It was around this time that Tom began using the Irish version of his name. He tried writing it many ways and decided that Tomás Mac Curtáin was the best translation – he used the Irish version of his name from then on.

After he left school Tomás's first job was with the City of Cork Steam Packet Company. Getting his first pay packet was very exciting as it made him feel independent. Not long afterwards he was approached by Fionán McColum of the Gaelic League. Fionán was teaching and organising the League all over Munster and badly needed help with his heavy workload. He had realised that Tomás was a great organiser and he asked him to give up his office job and start working for the League. Tomás went around with a grin on his face that could not be wiped off for days after this. He felt as if all his birthdays had come together. It was the perfect job for him and he accepted it gladly. He travelled all over the country teaching people Irish and organising branches of the League, but after a while he was exhausted and wanted to stop for a time. He needed a job back in Cork city and eventually got work at Mack's Mills.

Tomás's family and his friends were members of the Blackpool branch of the Gaelic League. When the regular teacher became ill, Tomás was asked to take his place and teach the class.

It was at this class that he met Elizabeth Walsh, who had come with some friends. From the first time they met Tomás was attracted to Elizabeth, but he was worried that he did not have enough money to

He travelled all over the country teaching people Irish and organising branches of the League.

support a wife. He also worried that too much of his time would be taken up fighting for Ireland's freedom, so he would not have enough time to spend with her.

Despite these worries, Tomás soon fell deeply in love with Elizabeth. Lizzie, as she was affectionately known, was five foot eight inches tall and had a strong personality. She too came from a republican background, and her father's side of the family were Fenians. Tomás dated Elizabeth for some time, but he knew that being young and poor he could not offer her much security. Yet to onlookers they were a perfect couple. One late autumn day in 1906, he took her for a walk along the Mardyke, a tree-lined pathway. At any time of the day there were always people strolling along this path, some arm in arm, some deep in conversation and others on their own, thinking their own thoughts and soaking up the peace and tranquillity of the area. Tomás intended to ask Elizabeth to marry him, but it took him a long time to work up the courage and even then he found it hard to ask her directly. Standing under a tree he said, 'I know a fellow in our office who is getting married on £2 a week. Hasn't he a nerve asking a girl to marry him on that?'

Elizabeth, who was more or less expecting the question, answered that she thought a girl might manage on it. The result of all their talk was that they came out from under that tree engaged to each other.

Tomás made sure before they married that Elizabeth was fully aware of his commitment to the cause of Irish freedom. He wanted to be certain that she knew how it would affect the marriage, but Lizzie knew of his contribution to the cause of freedom and was very proud of him. She believed that the public had only seen a few of Tomás's talents and that there was far more to this man than other people realised. Tomás had found a true soulmate in Elizabeth.

Tomás made sure before they married that Elizabeth was fully aware of his commitment to the cause of Irish freedom.

Surrounded by family and friends Tomás married Elizabeth in St Peter and Paul's church on 28 June 1908. The ceremony was followed by a small wedding breakfast and then Tomás had to return to his job. He was only given half a day off work for one of the most important events of his life.

The couple set out on their life together knowing that the path ahead would be full of difficulties and problems.

The couple set out on their life together knowing that the path ahead would be full of difficulties and problems. They moved into their new house near the Mardyke, which was a beautiful part of the city and only a short walk from the tree along the walkway where Tomás had proposed. Elizabeth always smiled when they passed it and remembered their special afternoon.

In the meantime Tomás continued to think about how to solve Ireland's problems. He thought that Ireland was too dependent on Britain and that the

British Empire had too much influence over what happened here. He believed that Ireland should be independent and stand on its own in world politics. However, it was hard for him to see how this freedom from Britain could be achieved. Irish trade depended on the British market and English was the main language spoken in Ireland. Tomás felt the Irish people needed to be made more aware of their past or they would lose their identity as a nation.

Tomás felt the Irish people needed to be made more aware of their past or they would lose their identity as a nation.

Tomás had studied Irish history and had learned that the British government never kept its word where Ireland was concerned. In 1907 he had joined the Irish Republican Brotherhood (IRB), an organisation dedicated to winning Ireland's freedom from British rule, using force if necessary. This was a secret organisation and its numbers were small. Tomás was an enthusiastic member and truly believed that a free Ireland was more than a dream and could be achieved.

Soon, however, he began to find it difficult to make time to do everything in a day that he needed to do. When a branch of the youth organisation Fianna Éireann started in Cork in 1911, Tomás became its treasurer. With this, and his involvement in the IRB and the Gaelic League, and his full-time job, it was hard for him to find time for family life.

Broken Hearts

Tomás and Elizabeth settled down to married life. They were delighted when they discovered that Elizabeth was pregnant and were overjoyed at the birth of a healthy baby girl. They decided to call her Siobhán – the Irish version of Suzanne – after Elizabeth's sister, known as Susie. Síle was born next and then a baby son, Patrick – named after Tomás's father. The house was a permanent hive of activity. In order to make things easier, Tomás took a new job as a clerk at Suttons, which offered him a better wage.

Unexpectedly, sorrow fell on the happy household. Their only son, Patrick, aged three, a source of great pride and joy, was struck down with an illness similar to meningitis and died on 25 November 1913. They were broken-hearted. Their world had been turned upside down and life would never be the same again. It was so difficult to explain to his two young sisters that their baby brother would not be coming home again. Every time Siobhán or Síle asked for him, Elizabeth was heartbroken.

On the same day that Patrick died, a meeting was taking place in Dublin to talk about setting up an Irish Volunteer Force. This group would defend the rights of the Irish people, and many of its members were from the Irish Republican Brotherhood and the Gaelic League. Tomás was very interested in attending the meeting, but he had stayed at home because of Patrick's illness.

There was further sadness when the baby that Elizabeth was expecting at the time Patrick died was stillborn just after Christmas. The baby would have been another boy. The family was devastated and Elizabeth found it difficult to recover from the sorrow. Tomás now worked until he was exhausted, hoping to forget his grief. It didn't work. He was also constantly worried about Elizabeth's health, but they both had to get on with life and look after their remaining family.

By now, the idea of freedom for Ireland had spread throughout the country. Speeches from men like Pádraig Pearse encouraged people to **Speeches from men like Pádraig Pearse encouraged people to take up this cause and there was growing enthusiasm for the idea of an Irish Volunteer Force.** take up this cause and there was growing enthusiasm for the idea of an Irish Volunteer Force. However, a talk given in mid-December 1913 in City Hall in Cork by Eoin MacNeill, who helped set up the Volunteers, proved that not all Irish people were ready to fight against British rule. There were many groups opposed to the idea of the Irish Volunteers because they were against the idea of using force to fight the British. In an attempt to stop MacNeill's speech, the lights in the hall were turned off to give the impression that the meeting was over. However, after the troublemakers left, the lights were turned back on and the meeting started properly. A committee was set up to start a Cork branch of the Volunteers and to admit and organise new members. The committee was made up of J. J. Walsh, who was its chairman, Diarmuid Fawsitt, who was vice-chairman, Tomás, who was the honorary secretary and Liam de Róiste, who was its treasurer. The group all had one aim in mind – to fight for the freedom of Ireland.

A committee was set up to start a Cork branch of the Volunteers and to admit and organise new members.

By 1914, the Volunteers had become a force that was not going to disappear. Tomás was now juggling his work for the Volunteers with his job and his home life, and it seemed as if there were never enough hours in the day to do everything that needed to be done. He was lucky to have Elizabeth because she acted like a personal secretary for him, keeping track of all that was going on.

Trouble in the Volunteers

Tomás and Elizabeth were now both very busy helping the Volunteers. Elizabeth was hard at work organising appointments, dealing with confidential documents and overseeing private meetings in their house. Tomás had been appointed to the military council of the Volunteers and this added to his already heavy workload. The Volunteers were divided into different companies, based both in the city and in the countryside, and Tomás paid particular attention to making sure that the units outside the city were not forgotten about or left out of any activities.

The First World War had started in the summer of 1914 and Tomás and his comrades were following what was going on in Europe with great interest. The British needed men to fight for them against the Germans and many Irishmen joined the British army. However, men like Tomás felt that they were needed at home to defend their own country. This difference in opinion led to a split in the Volunteers.

This difference in opinion led to a split in the Volunteers.

Those who followed John Redmond felt it was their duty to serve in the British army because of the threat that all of Europe would be taken over by the Germans. They called themselves the National Volunteers. But Tomás and many others were certain that the Volunteers should have one purpose only – to serve Ireland. They decided to stay and protect Ireland and kept the name Irish Volunteer Force.

Tomás was very upset by the split because he felt that the Irish people had failed to learn from the past. On many occasions Britain had been able to keep Ireland under its rule because the Irish had been unwilling to work together to win their freedom. Now he felt the same thing was happening again. However, that did not stop him enthusiastically continuing his involvement in the Irish Volunteers. The Volunteers were now training to make

The Volunteers were now training to make themselves an effective military force.

themselves an effective military force. Many men who worked hard all day in their everyday jobs then spent hours training on a voluntary basis, learning how to fight. Men within the different city and countryside groups were selected as officers to command their units.

English government agents had been watching the Volunteers closely and were becoming worried by this organisation and the threat it offered to British control over Ireland. Many Volunteers became afraid that they would be imprisoned or sent into exile. The British did banish a number of influential Volunteer leaders overseas, but a few important ones remained and helped to rebuild the Irish Volunteer Force (Óglaigh na hÉireann in Irish).

Many of the Mac Curtáins' evenings were spent in their kitchen with men like Terry Mac, talking about the actions of the Volunteer movement in the past, present and future, and looking at the possibility of a free Ireland. The dreamers, talkers, planners, thinkers and military-minded men all had a part to play and a voice to be heard. On many occasions Tomás went to bed with his head full of plans for how to make their dream of a free Ireland a reality.

On many occasions Tomás went to bed with his head full of plans for how to make their dream of a free Ireland a reality.

Both he and Elizabeth believed this dream would soon come true.

In the autumn of 1914, after the split in the Volunteers, the Irish Volunteers were officially reorganised. On 25 October a convention with 160 delegates from all over the country took place in Dublin and about a month later a 'General Scheme of Organisation' was published to lay out the military set-up of the organisation. As part of this, military units known as brigades were introduced and Tomás was elected as the commandant of the Cork brigade, with Terry MacSwiney as his vice-commandant.

Tomás was elected as the commandant of the Cork brigade, with Terry MacSwiney as his vice-commandant.

By November Tomás and his fellow leaders could see the benefit of their hard work. All the training had paid off and in a parade to remember three members of the Irish Republican Brotherhood who had been executed in Manchester in November 1867 (the Manchester Martyrs), the Irish Volunteer Force marched with great pride, impressing all those who watched.

When Douglas Hyde, the president of the Gaelic League, came to Cork on 15 December that year, Tomás thought it was great that both the National and the Irish Volunteers from Cork were part of one parade on this occasion: John Horgan led the National Volunteers and Seán O'Sullivan led the Irish Volunteers. Up to this point there had been a lot of rivalry between the two groups and they had not been getting on. Not long after this the National Volunteers would become part of the British army and be sent off to France to fight, leaving the Irish Volunteers behind in Ireland.

As 1915 began, Tomás and his comrades took their minds off the First World War for a time and focused on Cork. The reorganisation after the split had been tough and everyone involved was exhausted, but by now things seemed to be running smoothly again and the ordinary people supported them. The men knew their roles. Discipline and training were easy for them. The Volunteer pipe band was active and was often used in marches. Tomás had a beautiful set of pipes made for himself, with ivory tops and his name engraved on them. Elizabeth played the family concertina to him and the children at home, and when Tomás had any free time, he loved to accompany her on his violin.

Frank Daly, a friend of Tomás's in the Volunteers, feared for the Mac Curtáins' financial security. Tomás was now well known in the city and Frank knew that Suttons, where Tomás had gone to work in 1912, were unhappy employing a person who was becoming increasingly notorious. Tomás could be seen on a regular basis on parade and he was vocal in his views that the British had no place in Ireland. Frank believed that Suttons were about to ask Tomás for his resignation, or worse, that they were going to fire him. Then a building at 40 Thomas Davis Street in Blackpool came up for sale. It was made up of a shop opening onto the street, a mill and a flax factory to the back, and it had plenty of room for expansion and more accommodation than the family would ever need. Tomás and his brother Seán discussed the advantages of buying the building and

Tomás could be seen on a regular basis on parade and he was vocal in his views that the British had no place in Ireland.

were confident they could turn it into a profitable business. Although Elizabeth was reluctant to leave the home that she loved and the area of the city where they had spent so many happy times, she agreed that the move was right for the family.

So Tomás, Elizabeth and the children moved to 40 Thomas Davis Street to start what they hoped would be an exciting new life. Seán already had a large shop in Shandon Street and was a partner in this new business with Tomás. To start with things were not easy and money was scarce. On top of that some of the female

So Tomás, Elizabeth and the children moved to 40 Thomas Davis Street to start what they hoped would be an exciting new life.

workers from the flax factory, whose husbands were in the British army, used to stand at the family's door at night, shouting abuse because of Tomás's involvement with the Irish Volunteers. Elizabeth understood why they were angry but believed that they did not fully understand the situation. Tomás and Seán let these women keep their jobs despite their attitude and the fact that plenty of other workers were available. They believed that a fair day's work deserved a fair day's pay and gave the flax workers and the clothes factory girls what were considered very good working conditions. The manufacturing of clothes was an expansion that Tomás and Seán had introduced to build up the business.

Even though he had a new business to run, when Tomás had any spare time in the shop he would be writing notes, jotting down ideas, and sending and receiving messages for the Volunteers. The place was as busy as a railway station with the comings and goings of Volunteer officers who would come in to talk with Tomás. Elizabeth soon learned that it was wise to have a spare bed and an extra meal ready, as many of these talks went on late into the night.

Danger of Exile

Almost every hour of Tomás's days was now spent between 40 Thomas Davis Street and the Volunteers' hall on Sheares Street in Cork city centre. Elizabeth spent her time running the house and helping with the mill and the clothing factory.

Meanwhile, the British government increased its targeting of nationalists, men known to actively support the idea of Irish freedom from Britain. Their agents went about making life difficult for supporters of this movement and many men were arrested because of their involvement with the Volunteers. Tomás became increasingly concerned, knowing that it was becoming harder and harder for the Irish Volunteers to remain an effective force. J. J. Walsh, the chairman of the Cork Volunteers, was banished to England and prevented from returning to Cork under the Defence of the Realm Act, which allowed the British government to punish any person in Britain and Ireland who was believed to be acting in a non-patriotic way. The vice-chairman, Diarmuid Fawsitt, also faced jail or exile and decided to leave for America. Tomás was very conscious that the leaders were under pressure, so a fund was set up to support the families of exiles and prisoners.

Terry Mac now became the full-time Volunteer organiser for Cork city and county, and Tomás accompanied him almost every week on a tour of the district units. Bursting with idealism and enthusiasm, the two men believed nothing could stand between them and their passion for a free

Bursting with idealism and enthusiasm, the two men believed nothing could stand between them and their passion for a free Ireland.

Ireland. Pádraig Pearse was travelling around the country giving moving speeches. When he was in the Cork area he was accompanied by a well-trained and equipped party of Volunteers and, on occasion, the pipe band played.

With the success of Terry Mac's attempts to recruit more men for the Volunteers, there were now many recruits who needed to be trained in the fastest possible time. Training and the importance of following the rules had to be explained to the new brigade members. The idea of following orders and reporting for duty was strange for some of the recruits, but Tomás and Terry were strict about discipline and respect. They believed that following an order instantly could save lives during a fight.

Terry was very aware that both himself and Tomás were now being watched by the British forces.

Terry was very aware that both himself and Tomás were now being watched by the British forces. They were leaders who had a great influence over their men. Many people felt that the British government would soon make a move against them. Elizabeth worried for Tomás on a daily basis. Their house was constantly searched in the middle of the night, the time that would cause the most disruption to the family. Armed police from the Royal Irish Constabulary would arrive and everybody's bed would be searched. More often than not, their mattresses were tossed onto the floor and slashed. The sight of guns glittering in the light of the candles terrified the children. It used to take hours to settle everybody back into bed.

Their house was constantly searched in the middle of the night, the time that would cause the most disruption to the family.

The mornings following these raids were extremely difficult, as a routine had to be kept for the children and Tomás and Elizabeth had a full day's work to face despite their lack of sleep. The raids were especially difficult after the birth of their new son, Tomás, on 14 June 1915, but the arrival of this new baby boy was also a cause of great joy. The family had also expanded with the addition of Elizabeth's sister Mary's two children, after Mary herself died. One of the good things about the house in Blackpool was that there was plenty of room for everyone.

Easter 1916

The family celebrated the New Year with Terry Mac and as Tomás said, 'They could be well pleased with the growth of the movement.' The Manchester Martyrs' parade towards the end of the past year had given a very public display of how far the Volunteers had come, and the compliments leading republican Seán MacDermott had given them publicly during his speech, and also privately, made them feel very proud. However, they could not afford to rest and each leader was very aware that they were still ill-equipped and had a long way to go with training their men. Tomás knew that success could only be achieved slowly, one step at a time.

One afternoon Tomás rushed home to Elizabeth with the news that Terry MacSwiney and Thomas Kent had been arrested. Tomás had warned Terry Mac that he thought some move would be made after some speeches he had given recently. Terry Mac was held for just over a month. When he was released he and Tomás made arrangements for a St Patrick's Day parade. Tension was high and both men knew they were being watched constantly. Just before St Patrick's Day Tomás and Elizabeth's home was raided, yet again, in the middle of the night and Tomás was very concerned about Elizabeth because she was pregnant.

Tension was high and both men knew they were being watched constantly.

The couple was shocked by a record of events published in the *Cork Constitution* newspaper, which suggested that members of the National Volunteer Force had given information to the authorities that led to the most recent raid. Could this really be true?

Both groups had different ideas on what had led to the split in the Volunteers in 1914, but Elizabeth could not believe that the National Volunteers would actually report the activities of the Irish Volunteers to the British authorities, knowing that this would lead to house raids and arrests.

Tomás believed the newspaper reports were being created to cause a row between the different sides leading up to the St Patrick's Day celebrations, but he was sure that if trouble broke out his men would not become involved. He would do everything possible to ensure that the parade was peaceful.

With this in mind, he issued the following order:

Irish Volunteers – Cork Brigade
St Patrick's Day Demonstration in Cork City, 1916

Your Company is to parade at full strength, and with full equipment, and one day's rations, at above parade in Cork City.

The Brigade will be inspected by an officer of the Headquarters Staff, and special attention will be paid to the conditions of arms.

For train arrangements, enquire of the local stationmaster.

Companies will be met on arrival by officers of the Brigade Staff.

Officers will please note the following Orders, which must be strictly adhered to: –

(1) Any breach of discipline must be severely dealt with and not let pass unnoticed.

(2) On no account will any man leave ranks without permission from his officer.

(3) Any man using ammunition without an order, either before, during, or subsequent to this parade, is to be immediately deprived of his arms, suspended from the organisation, and case reported to the Brigade Council for investigation.

Note – The special attention of all ranks is called to above order.

(4) On arrival at Cork all officers will take orders from officers of the Brigade Staff, who will wear a Blue Band round cap.

(5) Any man under the influence of drink will

be considered incapable, deprived of his arms and equipment, and forthwith suspended from the organisation, pending trial by court-martial.

(6) Every Volunteer is responsible for the honour of the Brigade, and should bear himself accordingly.

By Order of Brigade Council,

T. Mac Curtáin,

Commandant

Elizabeth insisted on going to the parade with all the children and her brothers and sisters. She wanted to show her support for the Irish Volunteers and to be there for Tomás. She was sure that with wives and children present it would be less likely that any trouble would start. She was right. The St Patrick's Day parade took place without any trouble. The household at Blackpool ended the outing with a special tea. Elizabeth put her thoroughly exhausted, happy children to bed that night. They were delighted at 'seeing Daddy as a soldier'.

Coming up to Easter 1916 Tomás was aware

that there was something being plotted in Dublin by some of the republican leaders, including Pádraig Pearse, Tom Clarke, Seán MacDermott and Joseph Plunkett, but he had no details of the plan. They didn't include all the senior Republican leaders in their planning, because they were afraid that some of them might think that the Volunteers weren't ready to take on the British military.

On Palm Sunday, orders arrived from Dublin outlining Tomás and Terry Mac's role in the plan for rebellion on Easter Sunday. Tomás understood from his orders that there would be a landing of guns in Kerry and that he was to provide an armed escort for them. He was under strict instructions that information was to be passed on only to people who really needed to know. On 9 April, he told the relevant brigade officers about their roles. At first

On Palm Sunday, orders arrived from Dublin outlining Tomás and Terry Mac's role in the plan for rebellion on Easter Sunday.

the men thought they were going on an exercise, but the distribution of first aid kits and instructions to be ready for anything left them in no doubt that things were more serious. Although not sure of what was going to happen, they were aware that some real action was about to take place.

In Dublin, Joseph Plunkett and Seán Mac-Dermott had obtained a document which they called 'the Castle document'. They rewrote this British document, giving details of how the British authorities planned to crush the Irish Volunteer movement. Their document was intended to give any Volunteers who were uncertain about fighting, the motivation they needed. It was clear that there would be a fight ahead and the Volunteers were now determined to stand their ground.

Tomás received an order to have his men ready on Holy Thursday, but then he began to receive different reports. Eoin MacNeill, Chief of Staff of the Irish Volunteers, was furious that he had not been told the full plan for the planned rebellion at Easter and so he cancelled the original order sent to Tomás. J. J.

O'Connell was then sent to Cork by MacNeill with instructions to stop any action there. At the same time a ship called the *Aud* was on its way to Ireland with guns which had been sent by Germany, Britain's enemy in the First World War, to help with the fight. The Germans hoped that by encouraging a rising in Ireland they would force Britain to withdraw vital troops from the war in Europe.

In Cork, Tomás was receiving conflicting orders and instructions. He went to Mallow to meet J. J. O'Connell off the train from Dublin, but discovered that O'Connell had gone on to Cork city. By the time Tomás got back to Cork, O'Connell was at Terry Mac's house on Victoria Road. O'Connell, following MacNeill's original orders, took over command of the Volunteers in Cork and all planned action for Easter was cancelled, not only in Cork but also in the rest of Munster.

Pádraig Pearse and Seán MacDermott realised

that they had to get MacNeill's agreement that the rebellion could go ahead if they wanted to have the full support of the Volunteers and they believed that it had to be now or never. They discussed the situation with him and MacNeill soon felt that he had no option but to agree to go ahead with the rebellion, but he was still furious as he felt that he should have been involved in the planning from the start. MacNeill now sent Volunteer Jim Ryan to Cork to tell Tomás that the original plan was back in action.

By this point the British were aware that something was going on. A senior member of the Volunteers, Roger Casement, arrived in Kerry to meet the *Aud* and was arrested. The Volunteers' leaders in Kerry, Austin Stack and Con Collins, were also arrested and sent to prison on Spike Island. Without their leaders, the Kerry Volunteers could not take part in the rebellion. Then the

A senior member of the Volunteers, Roger Casement, arrived in Kerry to meet the *Aud* and was arrested.

Aud was captured by the British navy. While the ship was being led to Cobh, the captain scuttled her and the much-needed arms sank to the bottom of the sea close to Cork harbour.

It seemed like the rebellion was off, but then Jim Ryan arrived in Cork and confirmed that it was back on again. Tomás sent word back to Dublin that he would do what he could. He had Volunteer units marching all over the county, in full view of the British forces. Tomás usually planned for all possible circumstances that might arise and his men always knew he would have a back-up plan if things went wrong, but the whole rebellion was very disorganised. Tomás depended on getting accurate information and instructions, but this was not happening. He was back in command of his men but was unsure of what exactly he was supposed to do with them.

He had Volunteer units marching all over the county, in full view of the British forces.

When news reached Eoin MacNeill on Easter Saturday that Casement had been arrested and the *Aud* had been sunk, he felt that there was no chance of success for any military action over Easter. MacNeill called for all action to be cancelled again, but Tomás had already given the order for military action to go ahead in Cork and was worried that there would be utter confusion if he ordered his men to stand down again.

Tomás and Terry Mac discussed the situation. Although there were rumours flying about, they had no idea what was really going on in Dublin. Men were marching all over County Cork and Tomás wondered if they were marching to their deaths.

There was no clear plan and guns were in short supply.

There was no clear plan and guns were in short supply. Tomás felt he had no option but to send his men home again. The weather conditions were horrible, but men were sent around the county by whatever transport was available to tell the Volunteers that all prior orders were cancelled and they were to go home and wait for further instructions.

Elizabeth waited at home for Tomás. He had left the house on Saturday morning saying 'I will see you later darling'. At various stages, Volunteers arrived from outlying districts looking for Tomás. 40 Thomas Davis Street was at the centre of the action. The men's first stop was normally the mill and, depending on the urgency of their journey, they would grab a hot meal and head off to where Elizabeth directed them, usually to the Volunteers' hall in Sheares Street. As she was going to bed, she saw from her upstairs window a number of Volunteers going home. She thought manoeuvres were over and was expecting Tomás home. She waited for him throughout the night, but he did not return.

Elizabeth's brother Tommy had gone to Dublin to serve with James Connolly's Irish Citizen Army in the rebellion. She later learned that he had joined up with Connolly's men and was based at the corner of Sackville (now O'Connell) Street and Abbey Street. He was dressed in his new uniform and was on duty on Easter Monday. A group of his friends from Cork passed up the road and started kicking his newly erected barricade. When Tommy went over to stop them they recognised him and started shouting, 'well look who we have here – good old Corkie Walsh', calling him by his nickname. They continued teasing him, kicking the barricade and causing trouble. Corkie fired his gun into the air to scare them off. History would record that Corkie Walsh fired the first shot of the Easter Rising near the GPO. Very few people realised that it was fired into the air.

History would record that Corkie Walsh fired the first shot of the Easter Rising near the GPO.

On Easter Monday, Tomás had asked a young Volunteer to let Elizabeth know that he had gone to Ballingeary to talk with Seán O'Hegarty, the leader of the IRB in the area. He was worried about his men and knew that the British authorities would be well aware of the confusion that surrounded

Tomás knew that the authorities would have informers in the ranks of the Volunteers.

the rebellion. Tomás knew that the authorities would have informers in the ranks of the Volunteers, but he also had his own ways of learning what the authorities planned. In fact he was amazed at how easy it was to get information on operations the British forces intended to carry out against the Volunteers. Having a postmistress steam open letters sent to officials might seem a very basic way of finding things out, but it worked. Off-duty officials could often be encouraged to talk and give out secrets after a few drinks in a pub.

That Monday night he and his fellow officers had no idea that the Rising had taken place in Dublin, and it was only when he returned to Cork on the following day that he heard what had happened. On going to the Volunteers' hall, he received orders sent by Pádraig Pearse, saying that the Cork Volunteers should rise at noon on Easter Monday, but the order was strange, because it was written on a scrap of paper and not signed, just initialled.

Tomás was hearing many stories, all related by people who had heard them from someone else, and none from people who had actually been there, so he had no idea of the real situation in Dublin. He had no definite orders and there was no clear plan. In Cork, there were no arms and no men as he had sent them all home. He felt responsible for the future of his men and did not want to send them to their death.

He knew that after the events in Dublin, the British would know what to expect and would deal severely with any action. He decided that there was to be no rising in Cork, but the Volunteers would stay at their hall to defend it. Tomás issued orders that nobody from the British forces was to be allowed to

He knew that after Dublin the British would know what to expect and would deal severely with any action.

enter the hall and that force should be used if this was attempted. Should it prove necessary to defend and hold Sheares Street by force, it would be the first military act of defiance by the Volunteers in Cork.

Elizabeth got this news and was sick with worry as the hall was quickly surrounded. T. C. Butterfield, the Lord Mayor, and James Crosbie contacted Brigadier General Stafford to try to stop any British action in Cork. They hoped that Tomás and his men could be talked out of the hall and no fighting would take place. Captain Wallace Dickie was appointed to negotiate for the British and a meeting was arranged with Bishop Cohalan, who represented the Volunteers. The British authorities had refused to speak directly to Tomás. The negotiators sent word that they would like to talk to Tomás. They were told that he did not intend to start a fight but if any move was made against him and his men, they would be forced to defend themselves.

Word came to Tomás in the hall that a number of British units were outside and ready to attack if necessary. The Bishop and Captain Dickie reached an agreement that if the Volunteers' guns were handed over to the Lord Mayor or the Bishop, no action would be taken against them by the British.

Negotiations went on and it was eventually agreed that the Volunteers would give up their guns. However, the Volunteers insisted that the guns would remain their property and that the British could not keep them. It was also agreed that there would be no publicity and a general pardon would be granted to the Volunteers for their actions. Tomás and Terry Mac had no choice but to agree and they left the city to make sure that other areas knew what was happening. They travelled around Munster to let the Volunteers know what was going on in the city, but when they arrived back in Cork they discovered that details of the agreement had been printed in the

... if the Volunteers' guns were handed over to the Lord Mayor or the Bishop, no action would be taken against them by the British.

Cork Constitution newspaper, even though part of the agreement said there would be no publicity. Tomás understood this to mean that the British forces were going back on their word and felt he could not ask the Volunteers to hand over their guns without reassurance that they would be safe. Captain Dickie reassured him that although the British government could not be seen to be making an agreement with rebels publicly, they would keep to a secret deal on this issue. Tomás convinced Bishop Cohalan to accompany him back to the Sheares Street hall to talk to the Volunteers. Along with Lord Mayor Butterfield, he spoke to the men and they agreed to hand over their arms to the Lord Mayor.

Men left the hall, some to hand over their guns personally at the Lord Mayor's home and some to go home.

Men left the hall, some to hand over their guns personally at the Lord Mayor's home (now the Mercy Hospital) and some to go home. Tomás, Terry Mac and the other leaders were very disappointed at the developments of the week and they felt that they had let down the men in Dublin, but there was no point in fighting when they had no chance of winning. They were happy that the men were able to go home with an understanding that their guns would be returned when the crisis was over and there would be no action against any Cork Volunteer.

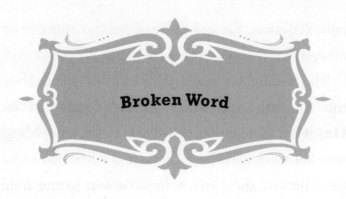

Broken Word

When he returned home, Tomás told Elizabeth not to worry. He told her about what had happened at Sheares Street and the various meetings with the negotiators. She was worried that he might be arrested and even shot. He reassured her that there was an agreement in place that Bishop Cohalan and the Lord Mayor had witnessed. He believed that the British authorities would not dare to break their word.

But Elizabeth was right to be worried. At the end of April General Sir John Maxwell, who had arrived in Ireland as military governor, ordered a crackdown on the rebels and the homes of Volunteers were raided. Tomás, his brother Seán and a number of other Volunteers in Cork were arrested.

The Bishop was appalled. He could not believe that the authorities would go back on their word. He set out to negotiate the release of the men. Many were released, including Tomás, but agreements had been broken and these actions proved to the Irish again that British government officials did not keep their word.

Although Tomás was free again, arrests were taking place all around him. Pádraig Pearse and thirteen leaders of the Easter Rising in Dublin had been executed. Thomas Kent of the Cork brigade was also executed. He had been captured on 2 May when the RIC went to his house to arrest himself and his brothers as part of the general round-up of Volunteers. The Kent brothers barricaded themselves in their house and

Pádraig Pearse and thirteen leaders of the Easter Rising in Dublin had been executed.

during a shoot-out with the RIC, Constable Rowe was killed and others wounded. David Kent was also killed and his other brothers were eventually captured. Thomas Kent was shot on 9 May by a firing squad. Tomás was devastated.

The British continued to round up not just Volunteers, but anybody who supported the idea of a free Ireland. Tomás felt guilty that he had not been kept in prison with his men. He kept going over and over in his mind the choices he had made, questioning if he should have made a different choice and if he had let down Pearse and the others in Dublin. Elizabeth's brother Jimmy tried to set Tomás's mind at rest by telling him that as a leader he had done all that was possible. He even enlisted Seán Mac Curtáin to reassure his brother and try to cheer him up.

Tomás and Terry Mac knew support for the Volunteers and their actions was growing. The people in the street were now talking about what had happened in Dublin. The executions of the leaders meant that the action they had taken would never be forgotten. Many now shared the dream of a free Ireland, and the horror felt at the death of the rebellion's leaders helped build support for the Volunteers.

The executions of the leaders meant that the action they had taken would never be forgotten.

Tomás was very unhappy with all that was happening, especially because young Volunteers were being arrested on a daily basis and this caused their families a lot of worry and distress. But he too would soon become a victim of the British. On 11 May, 40 Thomas Davis Street was raided again and Tomás was arrested in front of his family. The children were very upset and so was Susie, Elizabeth's sister. There was noise coming from everywhere as all the rooms were wrecked by the police. Elizabeth remained amazingly calm as Tomás was taken away, kissing him on the cheek, smiling and saying 'have courage'. These words stayed with him and, as he told her afterwards, were a great source of comfort to him.

Tomás was taken to Cork barracks, searched, and

his belongings were taken away from him, except for a little prayer book. He was kept locked up in the barracks and the only people he saw were other prisoners and his guards. When the prisoners met in the prison yard they were not allowed speak to each other and nobody knew what was going to happen.

On 21 May Elizabeth heard that they were moving Tomás and the men to Dublin. She sent word to as many relatives and Volunteers as she could contact. Early on the morning of 22 May all the prisoners were moved. Elizabeth, Susie and many relatives of the imprisoned men went to the jail gates. At about 8 a.m., Tomás and his men left the barracks to go to the railway station. They came out looking unafraid and Elizabeth knew they were putting on a brave face for their families. She did not get a chance to talk to Tomás.

Elizabeth was afraid that the moving of the men to Dublin meant that they were going to be executed. Tomás was a very important figure in the Volunteers and she thought that if they were going to execute more men Tomás and Terry Mac would probably be next. Soon she learned that this was not the case and that the men were going to be sent overseas to another prison. This news was greeted with relief – at least they would still be alive and there was

Elizabeth was afraid that the moving of the men to Dublin meant that they were going to be executed.

a good chance they would be released in the future.

Tomás wrote in his diary about what it was like in their Dublin prison:

We were kept waiting for a long time in the barrack yard. One of the officers in charge of us went to speak to one of the local officers and we were brought into a large hall or gymnasium and given some sort of tack [food] in a large bucket, bread and 'bully' beef. We lay down on the ground and ate it. We were then put into a big barrack room. I was in Barrack Room N1. There were twenty-four in the room and each was given three blankets and were told to sleep on the floor.

Conditions in the barracks were disgusting and Tomás complained that 'there was no toilet paper for us'.

On Wednesday 31 May 1916 the men were told to prepare themselves for a trip across the Irish Sea to England and a new prison. They were marched through Dublin and Tomás recorded that they were followed by a large crowd that had gathered. The people in the crowd started to shout and curse at the soldiers who were taking the men to the docks. As they travelled through the centre of Dublin, the men were able to see the destruction that had been caused by the fighting of Easter Week. There were bullet marks on houses and shops, and huge holes in walls caused by the big guns that the British had fired against the rebels. When they got to their boat Tomás wrote:

> We went on board ship at the North Wall and were put in amongst the cattle. I was afraid of getting seasick and I stayed in the air near the hold. Many more came out to where I was so

As the journey continued and the boat moved out
into the choppy waters of the Irish Sea more and
more of the men on board became sick. Those who
were not kept their mouths shut, trying to keep
themselves from being sick. Tomás was one of the
lucky ones.

When the boat arrived in Holyhead in Wales,
the men were split up, with some of them sent to
Nuttsfield prison and the rest to Wakefield prison
in England. Tomás was sent to Wakefield. The train
arrived at ten o'clock in the evening and the tired
men were examined and then locked up in cells. The
conditions in Tomás's cell were particularly bad and
he wrote:

The flagstones in all the cells were wobbly and
as old as the hills and were falling apart ... It was

BAD. The first day was bad enough and in the evening I got internal pains and as well as that I had diarrhoea.

He sent for a doctor but 'he gave me some stuff that only made me worse' and moved him to a cell across the hall. One good thing about his new cell was that Tomás got his meals first instead of last. This meant that instead of everything arriving cold, his meals were now hot when he got them. But hot or cold, the prison food was disgusting, so people who came to visit the prisoners, including the local nuns and priests, would bring in food and things like tobacco and sometimes even alcohol for the prisoners. In his diary Tomás recorded:

I asked one of the two priests who came in if he could bring in a naggin of brandy, having told him of the internal pains and being unable to eat. He said he would do his best. I sent many letters home that week to the people who used to visit us. A few days later the priest came in and gave me a bottle of brandy and when I went in after his visit I took a few drops and I felt improved immediately.

After being imprisoned for more than a week in Wakefield the men were told that they were being moved to another prison. This time they were to go to a place called Frongoch in north Wales. Although he was being sent to another prison, Tomás was happy to be leaving Wakefield, which he called 'a miserable, dark and unhealthy place'. Could Frongoch be any worse?

Frongoch

Tomás arrived in Frongoch on Saturday 10 June 1916, along with Terry Mac. When the men got off the train they saw a camp next to the railway that was surrounded by barbed wire. This was to be their new home. All around them curious locals watched the Irishmen. The camp at Frongoch had once been a distillery where whiskey was made. The buildings that were left had, according to Tomás, been made into 'one mighty spacious room, higgledy-piggledy style'.

Before they began locking up the Irish, the British had kept German prisoners captured during the First World War in Frongoch. After the rebellion in Ireland this seemed to be the perfect place for the British to put the Irish fighters, so the German prisoners of war were moved out of the distillery to make way for almost 2,000 Irishmen.

There was little chance of escape for the prisoners. The camp was in the mountains and the men were guarded night and day by British soldiers who would have shot anyone they caught trying to get away. Tomás wrote:

> The soldiers were equipped with shotguns and this was very sensible in my opinion because when fired the pellets would scatter in all directions and could do lots of harm, but with a rifle they would have to take aim and this takes time.

Clearly the British were keen to keep these dangerous Irishmen locked up and safely away from causing more trouble in Ireland.

Tomás was not the only famous Irish leader who was imprisoned in Frongoch. Michael Collins was also a prisoner there and they used to have long talks about what had happened in Ireland and how they could make things better in the future. They needed to keep the men in the camp busy and so it soon became like a giant school. Classes were set up and the men enthusiastically studied Irish and history. Tomás and Michael put the time to good use and began to plan for the future.

By the end of June 1916, some of the Cork men were allowed to go home, but not Tomás or Terry Mac. In fact, only two weeks later Tomás was moved again, this time to Reading jail in England, and Terry Mac was put in the cell next door. It was here that they got the news that Roger Casement had been found guilty of treason for his part in the rebellion and was to be hanged. At the appointed time of the execution, Irish prisoners in English jails stood still out of respect. It was agreed that all prisoners would stop whatever they were doing, be it work or pleasure, and pray for his soul.

Tomás wrote that night:

A newspaper arrived this evening and alas it

read Casement was hanged this morning. Bad cess to the English for perpetrating such evil, they are the devil incarnate. I am of the opinion that as true as God is above they will pay for it later. His final words from the gallows were, 'I am going to death for my country'. There were three priests in attendance at his execution and he died a Catholic. We were shaking with anger when we read it … Ruairí [Casement] was such a fine noble man – may God have mercy on him, Jesus have mercy on him and may he be seated at the right hand of God.

Elizabeth and everyone at home wrote as often as they could and made little parcels for Tomás and the men. Cakes were wrapped and sent. On occasion someone actually went to England to visit the men and food and gifts would be hastily put together to make a package. They also sent socks and jumpers that had been knitted in anticipation of a long, cold winter for the men locked up in their small stone cells. Elizabeth also had special photographs taken of the family to send to Tomás, which he showed the other men with pride.

Life in jail passed slowly and Tomás kept himself busy by reading. Autograph books were also passed around between the men. These books allowed them to write notes to each other to be kept for the future. Many of the men spent hours wondering what to write, while others took the books and spent hours writing and drawing in them. Tomás got great pleasure reading through his autograph book. In it was a sketch of his children crying for him, which he loved, as well as a drawing of Pádraig Pearse that he thought was exceptional. He treasured this book and knew that Elizabeth would enjoy studying the autographs when he brought it home. During all the long days he was kept in prison he clung to the idea that he would get home sometime, and he longed to see his wife and children again.

Tomás was always delighted to get news from home and read and reread all his letters. He missed Elizabeth and the children a lot, but he could not change the situation so he just had to put up with it. For Elizabeth back home, it was also a difficult time. She had her hands full with the children, and she also had a lot of work to do to keep the family business going. With Tomás away, Elizabeth was also very lonely.

Back in England, shut away in his prison cell, Tomás faced the prospect of a lonely Christmas, the first one he would ever have spent away from his family. He knew that his absence made life very difficult at home and he realised that the men would get nowhere without the support of the Irish women. It was

He knew that his absence made life very difficult at home ...

the women who kept the families going when the men were off fighting and in prison.

Back at 40 Thomas Davis Street, Tomás's brother Seán, who had also been in prison but had been released some time earlier, was helping to keep the business going – but the mill and shop were only just surviving. What was worse for the family was that even though Tomás was in prison, their house was still being raided on a regular basis. Elizabeth never mentioned this in her letters but he always found out. Some of the other lads who were in Reading jail with Tomás would get letters telling them about the raids on the Mac Curtáins' house, and they passed this news on to him.

Just before Christmas 1916 the British decided to allow many of the Volunteers to return home, but Christmas week came and still Tomás was not given his freedom. Elizabeth and the children had been hopeful that he would make it home for Christmas, but as the week went on it seemed less and less likely that he would. The children had been constantly asking, 'Will Dada be home?' All week long Elizabeth had said 'maybe', but that night as they went to bed she had been honest and said, 'No my darlings, not this Christmas, maybe in the New Year. He sends his love and he knows that we are all thinking of him.'

Christmas morning arrived and there was great excitement all over the house. Elizabeth had insisted that they would all go to mass before the presents were exchanged. Just after noon the gifts were unwrapped and they all sat down to a meal together. Later they sat around the table and talked until Elizabeth, her mum, her two brothers Tommy and Jimmy, her sister Hannah and all the children were tired out. Elizabeth smiled to herself. All in all things had gone well. They had enough money for small gifts for everybody and the children had had a great day.

A commotion at the door startled her. Jimmy went down to see what was happening. A group of excited Volunteers were outside and she reacted to the shouts of 'Mrs Mac, you better come down, Mrs Mac where are you?' Elizabeth hurried to the open door. Tomás emerged from the crowd of men and she was so delighted to see him that she gave him a huge hug.

When he entered the

Tomás emerged from the crowd of men and she was so delighted to see him that she gave him a huge hug.

house Tomás, who was exhausted from the journey, sat down in a chair and the children threw themselves on top of him. He told them that he had been let go only the day before, on 24 December. After a lot of travelling he had made it home to be with his family on Christmas Day and he was overjoyed to be there.

Life in Thomas Davis Street settled down once again. Business was not good and the mill was just about surviving. When the grain was delivered to the docks, the bags were slashed by soldiers with bayonets checking that there were no guns hidden inside. The sacks were so damaged that often, by the time Tomás took delivery of them, they were less than half full of grain. There was very little spare money around. Many households had their men away fighting in the First World War and were having to make some money in part-time jobs just to survive. The Mac Curtáins' clothing factory employed many locals and the sale of clothes was steady but small. It was strange for Tomás to be surrounded by the noise and bustle of life, having been locked away for so long, but Elizabeth and the children were happy to have him home.

Everyday tasks took over. Tomás and Elizabeth had time to talk and make decisions about the children's schooling. The accounts for the mill had to be checked and updated. Tomás liked to check every order, delivery and outstanding payment, so the work soon piled up.

But Tomás's freedom and the pleasures of home life did not last long. On 26 February 1917, District Inspector Swanzy arrested him again. He was brought to Kings Street barracks first. Terry Mac was also arrested and both men were moved to the military detention barracks.

Tomás was taken with Terry Mac to Arbour Hill prison in Dublin. Then he was sent to live in Ledbury and Terry Mac was sent to Bromyard, two towns in England which were quite close to each other. Though not surrounded by prison walls this time, this type of punishment was very difficult. It was definitely easier than prison, but the men were by themselves and very lonely. They were not locked up but they had to stay in certain areas of England and the English government would not give them any money for living. They had to rely on their families for survival. There was no chance of getting even a part-time job, so the women at home, who were already struggling to make enough money to live, were now forced to send their husbands money as well. Eventually, in mid-March, the British government gave in to pressure from the prisoners and their families, and agreed to pay for housing and food.

If they left the small area where they had to stay, the men knew that they would be arrested and put in a regular prison. Tomás spent his days playing music and reading poetry. On Easter Monday he went to Bromyard, which was at the outer edge of the area in which he could travel, and met up with Terry Mac and another friend of theirs who was there, Seán Nolan. They talked about the events of the previous Easter.

The amount of time Tomás was spending away from his family was depressing him. Later in the month Terry came to visit him and told him that he and Muriel Murphy were going to marry in

June. Muriel came from Cork and was one of the Murphys who owned the brewery in the city. Although they had no idea when the men would be allowed home, the couple had decided to set the date anyway. Tomás was thrilled with the news and they all looked forward to the wedding.

Meanwhile, Elizabeth's family decided they would leave their home at Moorfield Terrace and all move into 40 Thomas Davis Street. There were so many empty rooms that this seemed like a good idea. Elizabeth's mother was old and needed care, and her sister and brother could spend more time with Elizabeth and help her to mind the children as she was pregnant again. Her brothers and sisters felt that a new baby, along with Mary's children and her own children were just too much for Elizabeth to manage alone. The new arrangement worked well for them all. Tomás was relieved as he knew that Elizabeth was nervous in the house at night. This seemed the perfect solution.

The eyes of the world were beginning to turn to Ireland. The public supported the Volunteers and

The eyes of the world were beginning to turn to Ireland. the British forces were now under pressure to treat the Irish fairly. A strong interest in the fight for Irish freedom was growing in the United States, as many Volunteers who had gone on the run or were exiled had moved to the United States and were gaining support for the cause there.

Irish politics were also showing this change in opinion. The Sinn Féin party, which was the political party that stood for Irish independence, was now gaining massive support. One of its members, Count George Plunkett, stood for election in Roscommon and won easily.

Tomás and Elizabeth watched the event with great interest and were glad of Sinn Féin's victory. Sadly this good news was cancelled out by the bad news that the British had taken possession of the Volunteers' hall in Sheares Street in early June and closed it down.

Home and the future

The British government decided to reduce the length of many of the prisoner's sentences and on 21 June Tomás was back home at Thomas Davis Street. He went to have a look at the Volunteers' hall in Sheares Street but was disappointed to see that it was occupied by British forces.

Many of the people fighting for Irish freedom now decided that the best plan would be to get themselves elected. Count Plunkett had already had a great win and Éamon de Valera had another great victory in the Clare elections. Win after win for the republicans took place. This proved how popular they were with the Irish people who were voting for them. Normally men elected in Ireland took their place in the British parliament, but the newly elected republicans refused to do so as a sign that they were standing for a free Ireland.

In September 1917, the world's attention once more turned to Ireland, this time because of Thomas Ashe. In August Ashe had been arrested and sent to Mountjoy jail in Dublin for making an anti-British speech at Ballinalee. He was treated as an ordinary criminal prisoner, which he thought was unfair, and so in September he went on hunger strike to try and force his captors to treat him as a political prisoner. A few days later, the authorities decided to try and force him to eat by putting a tube down his throat and into his stomach and pouring liquid food down this tube. The procedure of inserting the tube went badly wrong and cut into his lung. He died

In September of 1917, the world's attention was once more turned to Ireland because of Thomas Ashe.

soon afterwards. This terrible story horrified not only Irish people, but people in Britain and America. Tomás led a parade of battalions of the Volunteers to honour the memory of Thomas Ashe.

Since the Easter Rising in 1916 the British government had forbidden any public gatherings of large numbers of men, including the Volunteers. Carrying weapons, wearing uniforms, or any group action like parading was banned. The Volunteers decided they were going to ignore this ban and would disobey the British government over this issue. On Sunday 21 October, all over the country, Volunteers met and marched together. In Cork, approximately 1,000 men met outside the hall at Sheares Street and marched all the way to Blarney. Tomás led the parade and Terry Mac marched with him; both men wore uniforms and were followed by their men. Most of the men did not have uniforms, but they used any bits and pieces they had to make themselves look like soldiers: some wore caps, others belts, others boots. Tomás was in no doubt as to what the result would be for this action: 'We knew we would be arrested, but something new was needed to raise the spirit of the people.' He was arrested and held for a short time in Cork jail.

Soon after this there was a big meeting with all the leaders of the Volunteers in Dublin. Tomás went to this meeting. He was only home in Cork for one day when he was arrested again with a number of other men. When brought before the court, Tomás spoke in Irish and said:

> I have not the slightest respect for this foreign court. Its ruling I will not follow, its laws I will not accept, and furthermore I will not speak its language. I will be true to the ideals of the men who established the Republic last Easter. From their deaths will come the freedom of the land of Ireland.

Each prisoner said the same thing. The judge was outraged at this display of defiance and sentenced each man to six months in jail, but by Christmas 1917 Tomás had been released and was back with

Elizabeth and the children. He was then asked by Sinn Féin to run for election in South Armagh just after the New Year. After thinking about this for some time and discussing it with Elizabeth, he decided to travel to Armagh and he asked any Volunteers who were available to come up and help him. He did not win, but he was delighted with the publicity he got for Sinn Féin and the Volunteers.

In March many of the Volunteers' leaders were arrested again. Tomás knew it was only a matter of time before he would be re-arrested and so he went on the run, visiting the battalions of Volunteers all over County Cork and encouraging them to continue training.

On 9 April, the British Prime Minister, David Lloyd George, tried to introduce the conscription bill to Ireland, which only made British rule in Ireland even more unpopular amongst the Irish people. This bill said that if you were over eighteen then you had to serve in the British army, which meant that every Irishman of the right age could be sent off to fight and die in the war which was still going on in Europe. Most Irish people decided to oppose the introduction of this bill in any way possible. If this meant they had to fight to stop the bill being introduced, then they were prepared to do so. With the end of the war in November 1918, the problem went away.

While Tomás was on the run, the police raided 40 Thomas Davis Street on a regular basis looking for him. Elizabeth assured him that there was no need for him to worry. She and the children were fine, and he was to stay away from the house as it was being watched by the police waiting to catch him if he came back. Elizabeth and Tomás had no trouble keeping in touch with each other because a network of Volunteers on bicycles took messages all over the countryside. When one was tired, another one took over and so the couple were able to send messages to each other regularly. Tomás's time was spent dodging arrest and going from safehouse to safehouse. During this time, he was still in charge of the Cork Volunteers and made sure he still knew everything that was going on, wherever he was. He was pleased with the organisation and with the skills of his men.

Tomás went home for a quick visit during Christmas 1918 and by January it appeared that the police were no longer looking to arrest the Volunteer leaders so he returned home to live. At the start of the new year, it was decided

In early January police barracks were attacked all over the country. The Volunteers wanted to take the weapons that were kept there.

that the Volunteers would become more forceful in their opposition of British rule. In early January police barracks were attacked all over the country. The Volunteers wanted to take the weapons that were kept there. In County Cork, they successfully captured the police barracks in Carrigtwohill. Also in January the Volunteers in the county were reorganised because there were now too many men involved over too big an area for Tomás to control them all. He was constantly travelling but he tried to get home as often as possible, or to meet with Elizabeth and the children in safehouses.

Because of the growing size of the Volunteers and their attacks on police barracks, the British decided to send more troops into Ireland to keep the peace. The British were very worried that they would lose their control over Ireland but they were determined to do everything possible to stop this happening. It was easier for them to keep control in the cities, and so their numbers there grew, including in Cork.

It was decided that the Volunteers needed people in important positions to publicly stand up against the British and argue for a free Ireland. Since Tomás was a well-known figure around Cork, he was asked to stand for election to the Cork City Council. This decision made the road ahead even more dangerous for him and his family.

Elections in Cork

Elizabeth never doubted the outcome of the election for one moment: Tomás easily won a place on the Council. Sinn Féin did well in the elections and it was up to them to select the new Lord Mayor for the city. Tomás was told that he was to be Sinn Féin's choice for the position, but he was afraid of what might happen if he was given the title of Lord Mayor. He had already received an anonymous written warning that if he became Lord Mayor then he would be killed. He was, after all, a notorious leader of the Cork Volunteers and was leading the fight against the British in the area. In the end Tomás felt that he had no choice and that if he was offered the job he would have to accept it. He looked on it as his duty as a soldier.

On the morning of 30 January 1920, the day of the vote for the new Lord Mayor, Tomás sneaked into City Hall at seven o'clock in the morning to make sure that he avoided the police who would have arrested him. When all the new councillors had arrived, they sat down to elect the Lord Mayor. Of the fifty-one men who were there, forty were from the Sinn Féin party, which meant that they had a majority and could pick whoever they wanted for Lord Mayor. Proud of their Irish history, they carried out the entire meeting in Irish. Micheál Ó Cuill proposed Tomás to be the new Lord Mayor and Terry Mac, who had also been elected to the Council, seconded him. He was unanimously elected and he accepted the position of first republican Lord Mayor of Cork.

He was unanimously elected and he accepted the position of first republican Lord Mayor of Cork.

Tomás stood to receive his chain of office. Elizabeth and her brother Jimmy were watching from the side and they thought they would burst with pride. His wife was immensely proud of the speech he made when accepting the role – he spoke of his wish for a free Ireland and asked that all the members of the Council should agree not to support the British government but to support instead the new Irish government that had just been set up, Dáil Éireann. Up to this point, the Lord Mayor had always reported to the British government. The new Cork Council members accepted the proposal. Tomás stood proud, wearing a Sinn Féin rosette, as, for the first time, the new Irish tricolour flag of green, white and orange was raised over City Hall. A new beginning for Ireland was coming.

It was also suggested at this time that the salary of the new Lord Mayor should be raised to £1,000. Tomás objected to this because he believed the people of Cork were in no position to pay him such a large amount of money. There were too many people who were going hungry in the city and he suggested that the money could be used to feed them instead.

It had always been a custom that the Lord Mayor could choose a spiritual advisor, who would help him in his role as first citizen of the city. Tomás appointed Father Dominic as his chaplain. Father Dominic had been chaplain to the Cork Volunteers and was a great friend of Tomás.

What a great day they all had! The Agriculture Show was on in Cork and Tomás had made an official visit as Lord Mayor. Elizabeth, the children and Jimmy had all gone with him, and his daughters had loved seeing their father driving a Ford tractor as part of a demonstration. There were squeals of delight as Tomás headed off to plough part of a field. The pipe band had played at the show and there was a relaxed and happy festive atmosphere. Tomás had to stay there for hours because everybody wanted to shake hands with the new Lord Mayor, but he was glad to do this and to meet all the people there. The family returned to Thomas Davis Street exhausted, but happy.

On the night of 19 March, Elizabeth went to bed very tired, but she knew that Tomás must be even more tired than she was. With all the changes and excitement of his new job it seemed like weeks since he had had a good night's sleep. She hoped he would be able to have a rest in bed the next morning. As she got ready for bed she thought about the plans for the next day. It was Tomás's thirty-sixth birthday and it was to be a special day spent with their children and her brothers and sisters. Everybody was excited by the prospect of the small surprise party that was planned. The cake had been made and hidden so that he would not see it and spoil the surprise. There were lots of presents: the children had found fun trinkets for him; Annie, Susie and Hannah, Elizabeth's sisters, had bought him books, and Elizabeth herself had purchased a silver match holder for him so that he would always have a match handy for lighting his pipe on the rare occasions that he smoked. Tomás had already promised to take the day easy, but she knew him better than that. Something was bound to come up, so she had planned the party for lunchtime.

Everybody had settled down for the night. Elizabeth's mother on the top floor was sound asleep, the children were in bed, and all was quiet. Elizabeth went up to bed at about half-past eight in the evening. She did not sleep, just lay and rested, waiting for Tomás to come home. He was late, but that was nothing new.

When he arrived home Tomás spent a long time getting ready for bed and stood looking out the window for a while. He did this every evening: the gas worker who was responsible for the city lights would pass below the Lord Mayor's window and give him a signal to show that everything was quiet in the city. On this night he was a little later than usual and so Tomás waited for him. He saw the gas worker nod and wave, and he went to bed thinking everything was fine. But what he did not know was that policemen in uniform, and some in plain clothes, were stopping people from entering the area of Blackpool where the Mac Curtáins lived. The police were slowly surrounding the area and making sure that the Lord Mayor's house was cut off from all outside help.

It seemed to Elizabeth that she had just closed her eyes when a loud banging on the front door woke her up. She jumped out of bed, telling Tomás to stay where he was. Hurrying to the window, she opened it a little and asked who was there and what was the matter. The only answer that she got was a loud voice shouting from below, 'Come down.' The shout was then repeated more urgently and loudly. Elizabeth quickly put on her dressing gown but because she was pregnant, she was slower than usual. By now Tomás was out of bed, and was pulling on his trousers and making his way to the bedroom door to go down to answer the caller. 'I'll go myself,' he said.

However, Elizabeth got out through the bedroom door in front of him and hurried down the stairs. She couldn't understand what could be so urgent that the Lord Mayor had to be called for at one o'clock in the morning. Her fear grew. As she reached the front door, broken glass flew towards her and the front door was almost broken down. She pulled the door open and a man with a blackened face ran towards the stairs shouting, 'Where is Mac Curtáin?'

Elizabeth answered, 'Upstairs.'

More men with guns followed him into the house, all with their faces blackened so they couldn't be recognised, and stood looking at the woman in the hall.

She pulled the door open and a man with a blackened face ran towards the stairs shouting, 'Where is Mac Curtáin?'

Then a commanding voice ordered, 'Hold that one.' Six men in total had now entered the house. Strange, rough hands grabbed hold of Elizabeth. Some of the strangers rushed past her up the stairs holding their guns. They seemed to know exactly where they were going. They stopped on the first landing at the door of the Lord Mayor's bedroom.

Annie and Susie had heard the commotion and had come down from their room. Susie was screaming 'Jimmy, Jimmy!' for her brother who had gone to bed earlier. Jimmy pulled on his clothes and put his pipe in his pocket, thinking that he was about to be arrested. He arrived at the door of his

He arrived at the door of his room just in time to hear a shout, 'Come out Mac Curtáin we want you.'

room just in time to hear a shout, 'Come out Mac Curtáin we want you.' He saw two tall men, one of whom wore a light coat, facing the Lord Mayor's bedroom. The baby, Eilís, was also in the bedroom, howling. Susie tried to push her way past the frightening blackened faces to pick up and console the crying infant, but she was ordered back out of the way. 'Please,' she begged, 'let me take the baby.' But her request was ignored and she was sent back upstairs.

Tomás was now standing at the door of his bedroom. There was the sudden sound of a shot from a gun and then another one. As the bullets were fired, the baby stopped crying. Jimmy, who had been making his way down from an upstairs room, blew out his candle, as he had not been seen yet by the black-faced men. He had no weapon and could do nothing to help his brother-in-law. Suddenly he saw the children. When Susie had shouted for her brother, five-year-old Tomás Óg and eleven-year-old Siobhán had heard the noise.

They were peeping through the keyhole when the shots were fired. He ran across the landing and signalled to the children to lie flat on the floor. He then rushed to the bedroom window and shouted for help.

He ran across the landing and signalled to the children to lie flat on the floor.

The black-faced men rushed to leave the house. A mixture of screaming and shouting could be heard as Elizabeth tried to get to her wounded husband. Some of the gunmen pushed Elizabeth from the bottom of the stairs out into the street and she was frantic to get back inside. She could hear her brother Jimmy shouting from the upstairs window, calling for help. The order 'fire' came from behind her, as the man in charge ordered a group of his men standing outside the shop to shoot. They pointed their guns at Jimmy and showered the window area with bullets.

Tomás was slowly sliding down the landing wall. A trail of blood was left on the wall behind him.

Inside the house there was total chaos. Elizabeth's sisters, Annie and Susie, had heard the shots and saw the backs of the men as they left the house. Jimmy had come back in from the window and went straight to his brother-in-law. Tomás was slowly sliding down the landing wall. A trail of blood was left on the wall behind him. Jimmy struck a match to provide some light on the scene. He heard Tomás moan, 'The children, Jim.'

'You're only wounded boy,' Jimmy said to Tomás to try and reassure him. By this time the children had run to be by their father's side.

Outside the gunmen marched away from the scene of destruction.

Elizabeth had known, even before Jimmy had shouted, that they had shot Tomás. A crowd had gathered in the street and she screamed at the people for somebody to fetch the priest. Peg Duggan and her sister, who were neighbours, took off running towards the North Cathedral.

Elizabeth rushed back into the house and up the stairs. She stopped at the top of the landing. Everything seemed to be moving in slow motion. Tomás's bloody body lay on the floor. Her sister Annie had her right arm under his head. Tomás Óg rushed towards her. 'Mama, they have shot Dada,' he said.

For a moment there was complete silence.

'Oh God,' thought Elizabeth, 'have they shot the baby too?' There was no sound coming from the pram. Then suddenly the baby started to cry again.

Elizabeth knew that things were very bad and that her husband needed a doctor as fast as possible. She grabbed the phone and shouted at the operator to put her through to the doctor. She quickly explained to him that Tomás had been shot and that she thought he was dying. Then she started to cry.

Annie gave up her place beside Tomás to allow Elizabeth to hold her wounded husband, and she prayed that he would live. Blood from the wound oozed slowly through his white nightshirt. Tomás Óg had pushed in between the wall and his father's back and was half holding his father's head. The warm blood that had come from his father's body was all down the wall behind him, and it stuck to his hand. It had a warm, sticky feeling.

Blood from the wound oozed slowly through his white nightshirt.

Annie ran to the bedroom and found the Lord Mayor's crucifix and his little prayer book. Síle was sobbing, while her Aunt Hannah hugged her, but there was no comforting her.

Outside, Father Butts from the North Cathedral pushed through the crowd that had gathered on the street outside the door of the shop. A path was made for him. He rushed upstairs to administer the last sacraments to Tomás.

The children were hysterical. Síle's crying was getting louder and louder. Máire was also weeping and the adults had to try and make comforting sounds to the dying man and attempt to calm the frightened, exhausted children. Eilís, the baby in the pram near the bed, screamed and screamed, and no amount of comforting would stop her. The house was in uproar. Tomás was still alive, but only just. He was murmuring to his young son and speaking words of love to his family.

All the adults who were there knew that he could not survive the terrible wounds. The family surrounded him and prayed for Tomás to live, but they knew that there was little hope. Elizabeth and her sisters tried to protect the children. Watching their father slowly die was not a sight they should have to see, and yet Elizabeth believed that the children should be allowed to spend these last few minutes of his life with him. Tomás knew they were there and this was very important to everyone.

After a short while, the Lord Mayor opened his eyes and looked up. He appeared to be looking a

He was murmuring to his young son and speaking words of love to his family.

little over the heads of his family and said, 'Into Thy hands O Lord, I commend my spirit.' Then there was complete silence. The children stood like statues, finally absolutely quiet. The priest continued his prayers, but made no sound – only his lips moved.

Tomás looked into Elizabeth's eyes. Showing how brave she was, she leaned forward and said, 'Remember darling, it's all for Ireland.' Tomás sighed and closed his eyes. His breathing became quieter and it seemed to become harder and harder for him to catch his breath. Finally he took one last deep breath, then it rattled out of his body and he was still.

The family could hear Doctor O'Connor rushing up the stairs and they stood back. Elizabeth moved to her husband's side allowing the doctor space to examine him. He told them what everyone was dreading. Tomás was dead.

The group knelt by the corpse in shock. It was almost impossible to believe. Tomás Mac Curtáin, first republican Lord Mayor of Cork, had been shot dead by the RIC. Two bullets had been fired straight at him from close range. One broke his ribs, while the other passed through his heart and then went right through his body. That bullet was stuck in the wall behind where Tomás had been standing. What was even more shocking was

Tomás Mac Curtáin, first republican Lord Mayor of Cork, had been shot dead by the RIC.

that the murder had taken place in front of the man's pregnant wife and young children.

The Lord Mayor is Dead

The family, who were gathered around their dead father, slowly began to move again. Elizabeth said, 'Help me lift him to the bed' and the whole family, including the children, helped carry the bloody body into his bedroom and set him gently on the bed. It was still warm from where Tomás had been sleeping just a little earlier. Elizabeth began issuing instructions to those around her, 'Annie, mind the children. Susie, check on Mama.'

Elizabeth then cleaned her husband's body and arranged him in the bed. He looked at peace. The family planned to spend the night praying by his side, but the terror of this night was not yet finished.

Elizabeth took baby Eilís in her arms to comfort her and went downstairs with Father Butts to see him out. He was still in the building consoling Elizabeth, when there was more banging on the front door.

'Excuse me,' Elizabeth said turning to answer the door.

'Police, Ma'am,' a voice announced.

'Are you going to kill my brother now?' asked Elizabeth.

'We have come to arrest Tomás Mac Curtáin and we have a warrant to search the premises.'

'My husband has just been shot and is dead.'

They pushed past her.

By this time, Jimmy was halfway down the stairs. Three bayonets were put against his body. He asked what they wanted, thinking they had come back to shoot him. They pushed him up the stairs. They repeated that they were here to 'search the whole house'. Jimmy asked where they would like to search first.

'My husband has just been shot and is dead.'

'Surely there is no need for you to still search?' Elizabeth asked as the men passed her on their way into the house.

'Orders,' was the gruff reply, as Elizabeth put Eilís back into her pram.

The team searched the house room by room. When they approached the main bedroom Elizabeth again stopped them.

'Don't you understand? My husband is lying in there, he has been shot and is dead. My family are at the bedside praying!'

She tried to continue protesting, but it was useless. The men pushed past her and Elizabeth and her family could do nothing but stand and watch as they searched the room. The police pulled up the mattress on the bed to look underneath and the body of the Lord Mayor fell to the floor, but the searchers did not care.

The raiders went from room to room, slashing mattresses and destroying the family's belongings. They even searched the children's rooms and Elizabeth's mother's bed.

The police found nothing and eventually left. They had been looking for weapons and for secret documents that would tell them something about the Volunteers. The only weapon in the house was Tomás's personal gun, and that was well hidden under the mattress in baby Eilís's pram, somewhere the police didn't think to look.

The raiders went from room to room, slashing mattresses and destroying the family's belongings.

Elizabeth tried to understand all the terrible things that had taken place over the last two hours. The house was now quiet, but the children were still terribly upset. Siobhán and Tomás Óg were the worst affected. Siobhán's hands were shaking like a leaf. Elizabeth called all the children to her and tried to comfort them.

'Dada is gone to heaven, please be good and Aunt Annie will put you to bed.'

Elizabeth hoped that tiredness would make the children fall asleep. The children went to bed but could not sleep. They remembered every moment of what had happened that night. Tomás Óg and Siobhán cuddled together. They cried and cried. When they did fall asleep, it was from exhaustion.

Not long afterwards a number of Volunteers arrived at the house to help out. They were horrified at the scene that greeted them, but they knew that there were some practical things that needed to be dealt with. Tomás's body was dressed in his full Volunteer uniform. The mess caused by the searchers was tidied up. The Volunteers set up a guard of honour and stood to attention at the bedside of their dead leader for the rest of the night.

The Volunteers set up a guard of honour and stood to attention at the bedside of their dead leader for the rest of the night.

Elizabeth knew that word of the death of the Lord Mayor would mean that there would be little time for the family to grieve by themselves. The next morning, before anyone arrived at the house, she gathered the children together to say a prayer at the bedside of their father. 'There is no need to be afraid. Dada is gone to heaven and we are all going to say a special prayer.'

The room was silent. Their father lay still and pale in his green uniform. His hands lay by his sides. There were six Volunteers in the room, three at each side of the bed, and it was clear from their faces how sad they were that their leader was gone. But it was nothing to the sadness felt by the children who had lost their father and Elizabeth who had lost her beloved husband.

The day after Tomás's death was a very busy one for Elizabeth. Because Tomás had been a very well-known figure and very well liked, her house quickly filled up with people from the press and photographers reporting on the shooting for the newspapers, undertakers arranging the funeral, and priests, city officials, republicans, Sinn Féin members, neighbours and workers, all of whom were there to pass on their sympathy to Elizabeth and the children. Elizabeth also had to deal with her upset children, as well as her elderly mother who needed looking after.

Everyone was concerned for Elizabeth. She looked

tired and pale. She was also pregnant, and people were particularly concerned for her health, as it had been a difficult pregnancy during which she had felt ill for much of the time. Elizabeth's family did their best to protect her from the endless questions and the decisions that needed to be made, such as where the Lord Mayor would be buried. Tomás's old friend Terence MacSwiney and another friend, Fred Cronin, arranged for him to be laid to rest in a new special area near the gates of St Finbarr's cemetery.

On Saturday night the city was quiet. Elizabeth stood at the top of the stairs wearing her black mourning clothes and watched as the body of her husband was carried down the narrow stairs. It was still less than twenty-four hours since the murder. The sound of the pipers of his much-loved pipe band and the marching of the Volunteers he had led could be heard outside. The body was being taken to the City Hall, where people from all over Ireland would be allowed to come and pay their respects to the dead man. A uniformed guard of honour surrounded the open coffin at all times. Anguish, sorrow, disbelief and anger were displayed by the hundreds of visitors and all over the city the people's sorrow was obvious.

Many people felt a need to travel to Cork to make their sadness and anger at the killing known. Throughout Saturday night and all day Sunday people from all walks of life queued for many hours to get into City Hall to mourn the dead Lord Mayor. They walked past his body in respectful silence.

Many people felt a need to travel to Cork to make their sadness and anger at the killing known.

The shooting of Tomás had a big effect not only on Cork people, but on the rest of the country as well. Many people who had not been interested in getting involved in the fight for a free Ireland now turned against a British government that could allow such a terrible act to take place.

On Sunday night Tomás's body was moved again, from the City Hall to the North Cathedral. Volunteers from all over Ireland lined the streets along which the coffin travelled. The men he had trained took the most active roles in the arrangements. The citizens of Cork crowded the footpaths to watch the coffin pass by, and no

The citizens of Cork crowded the footpaths to watch the coffin pass by ...

policeman or British soldier dared to show their face. Those who tried to count how many people had turned up found it impossible to figure out exactly how many were there, but they all agreed that there were at least 10,000 people on the streets. Never before had Cork seen such crowds.

Silence

On Monday 22 March, the day of Tomás's funeral, the city of Cork came to a standstill. The shops closed. Every factory stood silent. There were no trams running and the ships with their cargos floated silently in the water. The docks were empty. Nobody had been told to stay away, but nobody turned up for work. Instead they went to join the large numbers of people arriving in Cork to say a final goodbye to the Lord Mayor.

Elizabeth had an idea of what to expect at the funeral. Everything that would happen during the funeral had been discussed with her. She knew that Volunteers had come from all over Ireland and she thought that there would be a big crowd of people there. But even she was surprised by the massive numbers of people who had come to pay their last respects. When the mass was finished Tomás's friends Terence MacSwiney, Seán O'Hegarty, Joseph O'Connor and Florence O'Donoghue carried the coffin to the horse-drawn carriage that would take it to the cemetery.

Two black horses drew the first carriage, which was filled with flowers. There were so many of them that the entire carriage was filled and the flowers were trailing down over the sides almost to

Two black horses drew the first carriage, which was filled with flowers.

the ground. The carriage carrying the coffin also had flowers piled high on the roof. The main colours that could be seen were green, white and orange, and the coffin was draped in the Irish tricolour. Because the carriage had glass sides the crowd could see the flag-draped coffin.

A large procession of men walked behind the coffin, led by the young Tomás Óg. His Uncle Jimmy and godfather, Terence MacSwiney, were there to keep an eye on him and make sure he was okay. The procession was made up of Volunteers, men from the Council and lots of important men from all over Cork. They were followed by the Volunteers' pipe band. The citizens of Cork had never seen anything like this before and many felt that they had to walk behind the coffin.

The procession was made up of Volunteers, men from the Council and lots of important men from all over Cork.

The smell of flowers floated all around the procession. For such a large number of people the procession was strangely quiet apart from the music being played by the pipe band. When they reached the cemetery it too was filled with people all wearing black. Elizabeth, who was about five months pregnant, sat beside the grave for the long burial ceremony. She had slept very little during the night but tried to rest, concerned about the health of her unborn child. At the end of the service Tomás Óg, who had been sitting on her knee, jumped down and said he wanted to say goodbye to Dada. He went over to his Uncle Jimmy and watched as the coffin was lowered into the hole in the ground. Dada was gone.

Shots were fired over the grave and a heartbroken Terence MacSwiney spoke to the crowd:

> Although the great work, which has been done by the Lord Mayor of Cork, has been interrupted by his murder, the Volunteer Movement will carry on ... another will take our dead leader's place. No matter how many lose their lives in the course of their duty, as did the Lord Mayor, another will always be found to take the lead.

There were no long speeches at the graveside. Everyone knew that they had lost a great Irishman and for many of them, a great friend.

As the day drew to a close hundreds of people

lined up to shake hands with Elizabeth and to tell her of their sadness at what had happened. She wanted to meet as many of them as possible because she knew that a lot of people had come a long way to be there and she wanted to thank them, but there were just too many for her to talk to them all. Finally it became too difficult for her and the children, and they had to leave. They returned home to an uncertain future.

The Aftermath of the Murder

Once the funeral was over people started to demand to know why this murder had been committed and who had carried it out. An official inquiry, called an inquest, was held in the court in Cork into the death of the Lord Mayor, starting on 20 March, the day of the murder, and running to 17 April. A jury was presented with all the evidence and told about everything that had happened on the early morning of 20 March. Then they were sent away to think about everything they had heard and were to report back to the court with their verdict. They returned less than two hours later with a full report. They had decided that there could be no doubt that the shooting was not an accident. The Lord Mayor had been murdered.

The official report from the jury stated that they believed that the people who had carried out the killing were members of the police, who were acting on orders. They believed that these orders had come from the British government:

... we return a verdict of wilful murder against David Lloyd George, Prime Minister of England ...

We find ... that the murder was organised and carried out by the Royal Irish Constabulary, officially directed by the British Government and we return a verdict of wilful murder against David Lloyd George, Prime Minister of England, Lord French, Lord Lieutenant of Ireland, Ian MacPherson, late Chief Secretary of Ireland, Acting Inspector General Smith of the Royal Irish Constabulary, Divisional Inspector Clayton of the Royal Irish Constabulary,

District Inspector Swanzy and some unknown members of the Royal Irish Constabulary.

The report went on to say that the raids carried out in the middle of the night on people's homes were unacceptable, and it finished by passing on the jury's sympathies to the Mac Curtáin family for what had happened.

A number of times, as the report was being read out, it was interrupted by applause from people in the court. Everybody had felt that there could only be one verdict, but to have such an important figure as the British Prime Minister found guilty of ordering this murder was more than the majority of the crowd had believed was possible.

As well as the official inquest, Michael Collins, who was at this point one of the main leaders of the Volunteers, and who had been with Tomás in Frongoch, promised Elizabeth that the Volunteers would not rest until they had found out who had ordered the murder of her husband and punished them. The Volunteers knew that members of the

RIC had been the killers, but they had to find out exactly which members. Two men, Sergeant Denis Garvey and Constable Daniel Harrington, were thought to have been involved in the shooting. On 11 May, as they sat on a tram heading into town after work, they were shot and killed by a small party of Volunteers. The Volunteers also burned down a number of barracks across the county over the summer in retaliation for the death of Mac Curtáin.

Garvey and Harrington were not the only men to be killed for their involvement in the murder. The Volunteers believed that one of the main men responsible for the murder was RIC District Inspector Swanzy, who had arrested Tomás in February 1917 and been named as one of those guilty by the inquest into the Lord Mayor's death. Swanzy had been moved by the police to Lisburn in County Antrim for his own safety, but it did him no good. During the summer, the Volunteers found out where he was, and a small party of them went to Lisburn and on 22 August shot him dead with Tomás Mac Curtáin's own gun, the gun that had been hidden in baby Eilís's pram.

For Tomás's family meanwhile, life had to go on. On 21 April, a messenger arrived at 40 Thomas Davis Street from the City Hall at half past nine in the morning with a private letter for Elizabeth from Terence MacSwiney.

It said:

My dear Lizzie,

You see I'm not standing on ceremony with the death of Tomás R.I.P. My own responsibilities as Tomás Óg's godfather are in my mind and for that reason there should be no formality between us. I meant to write to you at once after the funeral to impress on you that any service I can ever be to you or the children I shall only be too happy to perform and shall look upon it even as a duty. You must never hesitate to ask me to do anything that is in my power to do. Even if the obligations referred to do not rest on me, my long and intimate association with Tomás through good fortune and adversity in our common work for Ireland has established a bond sacred in itself which would make me most anxious to help those he has left behind.

I am very sorry I could not write sooner – but I am chained here every day practically and have so many meetings and interviews. I don't know how you stand with the factory in Blackpool. But if there is any business matter relating to it that you would like to consult me on – you will of course tell me. If you would like me to call out there about anything – I shall be glad to do so but at the moment I hesitate to move in that direction beyond telling you of my readiness to bring whatever assistance I can. I hope you are all resting and recovering from the shock of your great loss 'though I know it must rest as a shadow on you always. Please give my best wishes to all and praying that God will direct and strengthen you in all things.

Mise le meas
Terry

Although Tomás was now gone, Terry Mac would

keep the dream they had shared of a free Ireland alive.

Terry Mac and the Cork Council started a memorial fund for the Lord Mayor's family. Donations big and small were coming into the office at the City Hall. It was the only practical way that many people could think of to help the family. Terry Mac himself had given most of his personal savings to the fund.

On 8 July, Elizabeth woke up with a terrible pain in her stomach. She had been trying to keep her strength up since the night of Tomás's murder for the sake of her unborn child but it had not been easy. The pain did not get any better and as the morning went on Elizabeth was in agony. She called her sisters and told them that they needed to call the doctor quickly.

The doctor arrived and Elizabeth was immediately sent to the hospital on Dyke Parade. At approximately twelve o'clock, Elizabeth gave birth, but the two baby girls were stillborn. Elizabeth was once again overcome with grief. Jimmy and Hannah buried the babies that day in the same grave as their older brother Patrick, who had died so many years earlier. The doctors could give Elizabeth no reason for what had happened. They baby girls had been perfect and their deaths could not be explained, but the shock and grief of her husband's murder had not helped her health and this could have been partly responsible.

A new Lord Mayor was needed for Cork and Terry Mac was elected in place of his murdered friend. Letters of sympathy continued to arrive for the Mac Curtáins from all over Ireland, England and America, showing how far the news of the murder had travelled and how many people it had affected.

A few months after Tomás was shot, on 12 August 1920, Terry Mac was arrested for possessing documents that expressed anti-British opinions and sent to Brixton prison in England. Shortly after he was locked up, he began a hunger strike to protest his imprisonment. His actions drew so much attention from America and other European countries that the British became afraid of what would happen if he died. King George V asked Prime Minister Lloyd George to find a way to end the hunger strike, but it seemed at the time that the only options were MacSwiney's death or his release. The British did not want to release him so instead they tried to force feed him as they had with Thomas Ashe all those years ago. Their attempts failed and after seventy-four days of hunger strike, on 25 October, Terence MacSwiney died. Another member of the Volunteers, Joe Murphy, who was on hunger strike at Cork jail, died on the same day.

The death of an Irish Lord Mayor in an English jail brought the eyes of the world back to focus on Ireland and her fight for freedom, and put the British government under increased pressure to find a solution for the growing problems they were facing in Ireland.

The death of an Irish Lord Mayor in an English jail brought the eyes of the world back to focus on Ireland …

Volunteers accompanied Terry Mac's body as it was shipped back to Ireland. As with Tomás Mac Curtáin, thousands of people gathered to pay their respects as the coffin arrived at the quayside. The plot of land just inside the gates of St Finbarr's cemetery where Tomás was buried was to be used once again and Terry Mac was laid on the right-hand side of his best friend.

After the death of Tomás and his best friend Terry, Elizabeth decided to move the Mac Curtáin family away from the house in Thomas Davis Street. With some of the money collected from the memorial fund that had been set up for her, a new house was found in 1 Grosvenor Place, on the north side of Cork, high above the River Lee. As Jimmy was still an active member of the Volunteers, the family were still in the middle of the action. The problem with this was that their house continued to be a target for raids by the police up until the time the family moved to Switzerland on doctor's orders to help Elizabeth's failing health.

Tomás Mac Curtáin, the first republican Lord Mayor of Cork was gone, murdered for wanting a free Ireland ...

Tomás Mac Curtáin, the first republican Lord Mayor of Cork was gone, murdered for wanting a free Ireland, but his story would never be forgotten. History would record the life and death of a soldier, a man of courage who believed in fighting for his country. The people of Cork would remember the leader and neighbour that they had grown to know and respect, and his family would always love and remember their father, who gave his life for Ireland.

Also in the Series

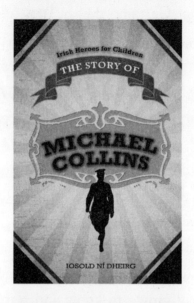

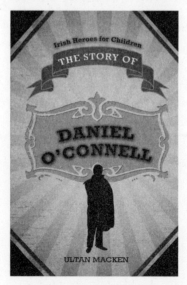